Make, Create, Celebrate!

Jewish Holidays through Art

by Julie Wohl

BEHRMAN HOUSE
www.behrmanhouse.com

Design: Elynn Cohen
Project Editor: Ann D. Koffsky
Editorial Consultants: Liz Diament, Tova Speter, and Diane Zimmerman
Copyright © 2018 Behrman House Publishers
Published by Behrman House, Inc.
Millburn, NJ 07041
ISBN 978-0-87441-972-6
Library of Congress Cataloging-in-Publication Data

Names: Wohl, Julie Schwartz, 1979–author.
Title: Make, create, celebrate! : Jewish holidays through art / by Julie Wohl.
Description: Springfield, NJ : Behrman House, [2018]
Identifiers: LCCN 2017036048 | ISBN 9780874419726
Subjects: LCSH: Fasts and feasts—Judaism—Juvenile literature.
Classification: LCC BM690 .W585 2018 | DDC 296.4/3
—dc23 LC record available at https://lccn.loc.gov/2017036048

Printed in the United States of America

The publisher gratefully acknowledges the following sources of photographs and images: (B=bottom, C= center, L=left, R=right, T=top)
COVER: SHUTTERSTOCK.com: anna42f(mask), Jacky Brow(menorah), greiss design(dove, shofar, honey, apple, pomegranate), Moljavka(candles), Medvedyk(etrog), Lucia Fox (lulav), xpixel (brush). INTERIOR: SHUTTERSTOCK.com: Elizaveta Ruzanova(palette), suok(camera), Yellow Stocking(GTK splash), Beyla Balla(paint), xpixel (brush),2, alanadesign 1C, greiss design 1, 71TL, 94, samritk 3, 52L, 53R, Yoki5270 3, vector illustration 4, dolphyn 5T, 5B, mimit2007 5R, Zagory 9T,76L,76R, LiliGraphie 9B, 64, 65, wowomnom 10, 77, Keep Calm and Vector 10, Danylo Staroshchuk 13T, 72, Elinorka 14B, 58L, 60, RozKah 15T, Yulia Buchatskaya 16B, Bystrov 18T, 18B, wildfloweret 18M, Noppanun K 19T, From the Sukkah City design competition, 2010, 19R, ToBeeLife 20T, 20B, RetroClipArt 22M, happydancing 25, Moljavka 28L, Markovka 26L, 27R, 29R, 50L, 51R, TWStock 32T, 33T, Elizaveta Ruzanova 32B, 33B, 40TL, 49M, 51, 55L, 60, 68, 75, 80T, 85, Nucleartist 36R, cosma 37, lyeyee 40L, JohnDakapu 40T, MIKHAIL GRACHIKOV 42,43, KellyNelson 46, Alfmaler 48B, Quang Ho 54L, AVS-Images 60M, Victor Moussa 60L, Lora Sutyagina 61, Shavlovskiy 62, Niall O'Donoghue, museyushaya 67T, Prokhorovich 70, girafchik 71T, UpicL 73, Ramona Kaulitzki 75BR, Yakov Oskanov 77L, CHANSIP SILARAT 79, Lucky-photographer 80R, Bipsun 80L, 80R, tomertu 82T, yul 82B, Titus and Co 83R, VerisStudio 85, naoto sonda 86M, TWStock 86L, 86R, Netkoff 89, Zekka 91, Jacky Brow 94B, anna42f 94R, Nicolai Ivanovici 96. Wikimedia Commons: Marc Chagall, Mrs. Simon Guggenheim Fund, MOMA 6; Wassily Kandinsky, Musee National d'Art Moderne 12; Fractured Bubble by Henry Grosman and Babak Bryan 19m; Tom Friedman Studio 22; Henry Rousseau, Gift of Mrs. Simon Guggenheim, Museum of Modern Art 18R; Ansel Adams 55B; Ernest Normand 58T; Proposition 8 protest 63; Moshe Castel 66; Menashe Kadishman, Jewish Museum Berlin 74; Yael Portugheis 83; Robert Delauney 88. Other: Julie Wohl 7M, 14, 18M, 30, 72L; Courtesy of The Jewish Museum: Gift of Dr. Harry G. Friedman 11B, 38B; Courtesy of The Library of The Jewish Theolog-ical Seminary 26TR; Freddie Levin 29M; Bezalel Workshops, The Jewish Museum: Gift of the Max Korshak Collection 32T; ©Yoram Raanan 2017 38; Louis Comfort Tiffany, Gift of Robert Koch, 2002, Metropolitan Museum of Art 44; Tree of Life Textile, Gift of Irwin Untermyer, 1964, Metropolitan Museum of Art 48; Karla Gudeon 50R; Susan Gardner(art), Jonathan Strahs (photo) 78.

CONTENTS

Ready, Set, Make Your Mark!

Welcome!

This is a different kind of book. It is a combination of a Jewish
holiday resource guide and an art journal. Feel free to respond to ideas
by writing, drawing, painting, or tearing to your heart's content.

Not an artist? Don't worry about it! This is a book about self-expression and ideas.
There is no need to make everything beautiful or perfect. As long as you are thoughtful
in your responses, you are good to go! And if you want some techniques and tips, in each
chapter there are suggestions for how-to videos that you can watch. You can find all
these video links at www.behrmanhouse.com/makecreate.

Inside, you'll find art, Jewish texts and stories, and new ideas on every page
that can inspire you and encourage your own personal creativity.

By the time you have completed this book you will have a record of your work and
a journal filled with personal meaning.

Most importantly, this book gives you space to have fun and be creative!

So, how will you do it?

They say the hardest thing about creating is making the first mark. So, let's
get that out of the way, shall we? Using markers, crayons, or oil pastels, fill
the corners of this page with shapes, doodles, squiggly lines, Hebrew
letters, your name in bubble letters—whatever you want.
It's time to make your mark!

Emojis of the Jewish Year

In the wheel, you can see a list of the Hebrew months and the Jewish holidays that fall in those months. Add at least one emoji next to every month in which a Jewish holiday falls; you can add emojis for the other months as well. Create emojis that reflect your own understanding and feelings about the holidays.

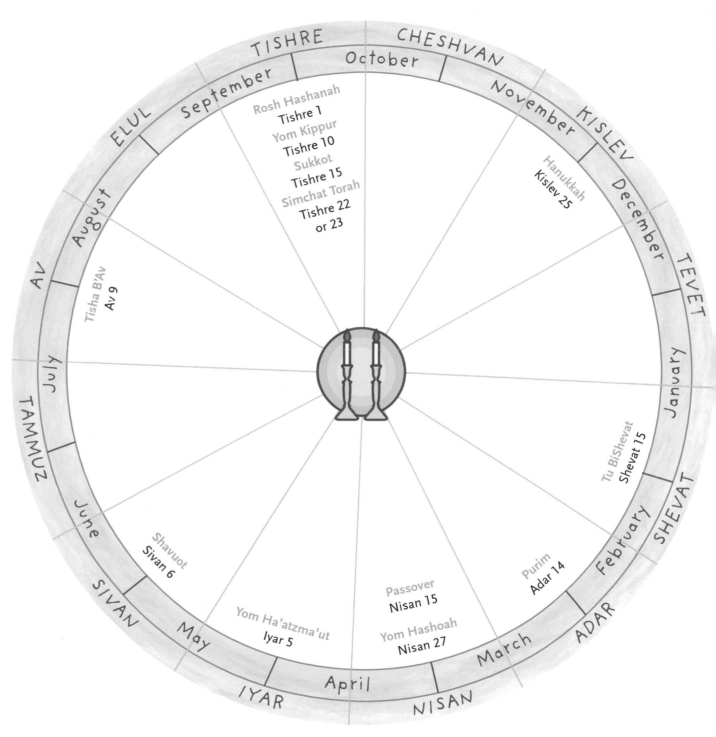

TISHRE

CHESHVAN

KISLEV

TEVET

SHEVAT

ADAR

NISAN

IYAR

SIVAN

TAMMUZ

AV

ELUL

September

October

November

December

January

February

March

April

May

June

July

August

Rosh Hashanah
Tishre 1
Yom Kippur
Tishre 10
Sukkot
Tishre 15
Simchat Torah
Tishre 22
or 23

Hanukkah
Kislev 25

Tu BiShevat
Shevat 15

Purim
Adar 14

Passover
Nisan 15

Yom Hashoah
Nisan 27

Yom Ha'atzma'ut
Iyar 5

Shavuot
Sivan 6

Tisha B'Av
Av 9

1 ROSH HASHANAH and YOM KIPPUR
Reflection

ROSH HASHANAH and YOM KIPPUR are known as the High Holidays. On Rosh Hashanah we are taught that the world begins anew, and so do we. On the ten days between Rosh Hashanah and Yom Kippur, we focus on the ways in which we want to grow and change. Finally, on Yom Kippur, we go through the process of *t'shuvah,* which means "return." We try to return to our best selves.

Gallery Tour

During his lifetime, Marc Chagall (1887–1985) was known as the world's most important Jewish artist. This piece shows his native village in Russia.

Take a look at this painting.

What do you notice? _____

_____

What is unusual about this painting? _____

_____

I and the Village by Marc Chagall, 1911

Chagall divided the painting into different sections. What did he put into each section? _____

_____

Chagall included a portrait of his own face. In what ways is his painted portrait different than a photo? _____

_____

My Selfie Story

About Art

Artists have painted self-portraits and created "selfies" for hundreds of years. When artists create self-portraits, they are using their art to share something about themselves.

On the High Holidays we are asked to do *t'shuvah*—to make some changes in our lives. The first step of *t'shuvah* is to really look at ourselves. Think about who you are to-day and what is important to you.

Consider the following:

1 Where do you live (in a neighborhood with lots of nature or in a big city)?

2 Who are the people with whom you surround yourself (friends, family)?

3 What activities do you enjoy doing (painting, reading, playing sports, dancing, acting, singing)?

Now try to express those ideas by drawing your own selfie or self-portrait. On the next page you will see a space divided by a large "X," similar to how Chagall divided his painting. Inside the large section on the right, draw a self-portrait like Chagall did. In the large section on the opposite side, draw a portrait of a person or animal that is important to you. On the top, create your setting—where you live or a place you love to be. In the bottom section, add details that show things about who you are—what you love to do or how you spend your time.

Think About

In what ways can thinking about our actions help us to become the best versions of ourselves?

Communal Prayers

We recite the Ashamnu and Al Chet prayers as a community on Yom Kippur. In both prayers, we list the ways that we have not met our goals during the past year. The prayers are written in the plural, to show that WE all make mistakes, and that WE all learn from our mistakes together.

Ashamnu

Ashamnu is a prayer that is structured according to the Hebrew *alef bet*. Here are the first few words of Ashamnu:

Ashamnu אָשַׁמְנוּ—We have done what we were not supposed to do

Bagadnu בָּגַדְנוּ—We have hurt others

Gazalnu גָּזַלְנוּ —We have taken what is not ours

Dibarnu dofi דִּבַּרְנוּ דֹפִי—We have told lies about others

Compose a modern verse of the Ashamnu prayer that applies to your life today. Write it in the space below.

_____

_____

_____

Think About

How can your friends help you improve yourself? How can you support others who are trying to change?

Once the whole class has completed their verses, post them in your classroom. Then, copy or add a photo of the whole classroom prayer here:

Our Community Prayer

About Art

An acrostic is a poem in which the first letter of each line spells out one or more words, a name, or a list of the letters of the alphabet.

Al Chet

In the Al Chet prayer we express ways that we have missed the mark. Recognizing that we have made mistakes is the first step of *t'shuvah*.

Working in groups of at least three people, create a dramatic pose, a tableau, that represents the relationship of Al Chet (missing the mark) to *t'shuvah* (fixing it). Choose one of the following ways that people often "miss the mark," and think about what you would do to fix it. In your tableau, some people can make the mistake, and others can show a way to fix it.

- *Al Chet,* for being wasteful
- *Al Chet,* for hurting a friend's feelings
- *Al Chet,* for being mean
- *Al Chet,* for being greedy
- *Al Chet,* for _____ (add your own idea here)

When you are ready, create your tableau and hold it. Ask a friend to take a photograph of your group's tableau. Then, print it out and paste it above or make a drawing of it.

Our T'shuvah Tableau was about: _____

Can you think of one way you have missed the mark this year? If you feel comfortable doing so, share it here: _____

_____

How might you do *t'shuvah*? _____

A tableau is a dramatic exercise in which a group of people create a scene from a story or history. Once the group creates their scene, they stay completely still, so that they look like a photograph.

The Magid of Dubno's Shofar Story

Pick volunteers, and read the story below aloud.

Narrator 1: Jacob ben Wolf Kranz, the Magid of Dubno, was a traveling rabbi who used stories to teach lessons. He once told this story:

Narrator 2: Once, there was a peasant who came to a town just as a fire broke out. He was surprised to see a number of villagers beating drums in response to the fire.

Peasant: (to small child). Hey kid, why are people beating drums in the town square while a fire is raging?!

Small child: They beat the drums to put out the fire!

Peasant: That's amazing! I must get one of those magic, fire-extinguishing drums for my own village!

Narrator 1: The peasant immediately went to a nearby shop to purchase one of the amazing drums that could put out fire.

Narrator 2: A year later, a fire broke out in the peasant's village.

Readers Theater is an activity in which readers read a script aloud, and the audience imagines the scene based on what they hear. In Readers Theater, there is no need for props, sets, costumes, or memorized lines.

Peasant: Never fear! There is no need to put out the flames, for I have a special drum that will put out the fire!

Narrator 1: The peasant beat the drum as loud and as fast as he could, but the fire did not go out. Soon the townspeople began to shout and cry.

Townspeople: Are you crazy?! Your drums may call our attention to the fire. They may sound the warning. But if we don't act, our whole village will burn!

Narrator 2: And so, the townspeople put out the fire, and the peasant learned this lesson: A drum can alert the town of the need for help, but it is only when the people act that the fire can be put out.

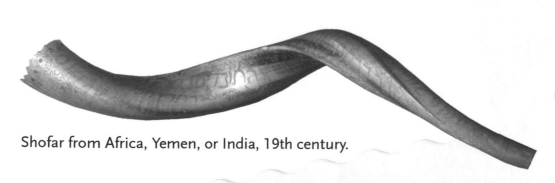

Shofar from Africa, Yemen, or India, 19th century.

Think About

How is the drum in this story like a shofar?

11

Visualizing the Shofar's Blasts

Like the sound of the drum in the story, the shofar's blast is a call to action. It is loud and shrill, like an alarm. It is meant to wake us up and remind us to reflect on our behaviors and make positive changes in our actions.

Gallery Tour

Wassily Kandinsky (1866–1944) was a Russian artist. He created abstract paintings that were often described as visual music.

Yellow, Red, Blue by Wassily Kandinsky, 1925

Look at this painting.

Imagine that different sounds are coming from the painting.

Where do you imagine that they begin and end? _____

_____

Which sections seem to be loud? Which are quiet? _____

_____

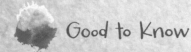 Good to Know

There are four types of shofar blasts that are played throughout the Rosh Hashanah and Yom Kippur services. Each shofar blast has a different tempo and beat.

T'ki'ah: A long, one-note blast ———

Sh'varim: Three medium blasts – – –

T'ru'ah: Nine short, staccato blasts ---------

T'ki'ah G'dolah: One extra-long, single blast that is as long as the shofar blower is able to hold it. ———————

In the box below, create a work of art that represents the shofar's blasts. First, listen to a set of shofar blasts either live, or on the video at www.behrmanhouse.com/makecreate. Then, create marks that represent what you feel when you hear each of the shofar blasts. Feel free to add to your work using colors and shapes, in a style similar to Kandinsky's. You might choose to add words and phrases to your artwork that connect to the idea of *t'shuvah*. You can complete this work with markers, oil pastels, or crayons.

My Artist Statement

This piece is titled: _____

This piece is about: _____

I particularly liked using these images/words/elements: _____

because: _____

Peer Review

Ask a friend to respond to your artwork.

Name: _____

I noticed: _____

I appreciated: _____

I learned: _____

▶ VIDEO LINK: Hear the Shofar

FINAL REFLECTION

Look back at the work you created in this chapter.

Which piece of art did you most connect with or enjoy?

Which ideas appealed to you the most? Why?

How did creating the art in this chapter lead you to think differently about Rosh Hashanah and Yom Kippur?

SUKKOT
Protection

"Shelter us in your sukkah of peace."
—from the Hashkiveinu prayer

JUST AFTER they received the Torah, the Israelites wandered in the desert without a home, relying on simple booths (*sukkot*) for protection. Sukkot is the eight-day festival that celebrates that journey. During Sukkot we build our own fragile, temporary outdoor booth called a sukkah. We eat our meals inside of it and try to make it feel as much like a home as possible.

Gallery Tour

Julie Wohl (born in 1979) is an American artist, a Jewish educator, and the author of this book!

Sukkot Party by Julie Wohl

Take a look at this painting.

What do you notice? _____

_____

What adjectives would you use to describe the atmosphere in this work of art?

Which Jewish symbols do you recognize in this painting?

_____

_____

Sukkah Word Cloud

In the cloud below, use words that describe Sukkot. Try different writing styles like bubble letters, cursive writing, curlicues, and all CAPITALS to personalize your cloud.

About Art

A word cloud is an image made up of different words, all relating to the same theme or idea. The words can vary in size or frequency.

When you visit a sukkah, before you eat a meal or a snack, you can recite the following blessing:

בָּרוּךְ אַתָּה, יְיָ אֱלֹהֵינוּ, מֶלֶךְ הָעוֹלָם, אֲשֶׁר קִדְּשָׁנוּ בְּמִצְוֹתָיו וְצִוָּנוּ לֵישֵׁב בַּסֻּכָּה.

Praised are You, Adonai our God, Ruler of the world, who makes us holy with commandments and commands us to sit in the sukkah.

Good to Know

Did you know that the American holiday of Thanksgiving was modeled after Sukkot?

Welcoming Guests

During the festival of Sukkot, a family's sukkah can be like a second home. Some people decorate their sukkah with fruits and vegetables, use beautifully dyed fabrics for the walls, or make art projects and hang them from their sukkah's ceiling. One of the nicest ways to make a sukkah feel like home is by setting a beautiful table inside it, and by enjoying a meal with family and guests. Today it's an enjoyable thing; in ancient times inviting and hosting guests was essential for travelers who were far from home.

Spiritual Guests: Ushpizin and Ushpizot

We invite our male and female biblical ancestors to be our spiritual guests (*ushpizin* and *ushpizot*) each night of Sukkot: Abraham, Isaac, Jacob, Joseph, Moses, Aaron, and David; along with Sarah, Miriam, Deborah, Hannah, Abigail, Huldah, and Esther. We welcome them to our *sukkot* and express our hope that their exceptional personalities will serve as inspiration and role models for us.

About Art

A collage is a work of art created by combining a variety of visual elements. It is usually created by cutting and pasting together found images, words, scraps of paper, and other materials to create one unified work of art.

Think about a person you would like to invite into your sukkah. This person may be someone you know or someone from history. Create a collage that describes that person and the values they can bring into your sukkah. Cut words and images you find online or in old publications, and glue them on the next page.

Living Jewish Values

The Jewish value of *hachnasat orchim* teaches that we should welcome our guests and make them feel at home.

My Artist Statement

This piece is titled: _____

This piece is about: _____

I chose to invite _____ to my Sukkah because: _____

_____

Peer Review

Ask a friend to respond to your artwork.

Name: _____

I noticed: _____

I appreciated: _____

I learned: _____

VIDEO LINK: Creating a Collage

The Lulav and the Etrog

What we call a *lulav* is not just a *lulav*; it is actually three different species that are held together: the *lulav* (palm), *aravah* (willow), and *hadas* (myrtle). On Sukkot, we take them, along with the *etrog* (a lemon-like fruit, in English a *citron*), and shake them in all directions to express the idea that God is all around us, providing us with protection from all sides.

Shaking the Lulav

1 Holding the *lulav* and the *etrog* (stem, *pitam*, facing down), recite the blessing:

בָּרוּךְ אַתָּה, יְיָ אֱלֹהֵינוּ, מֶלֶךְ הָעוֹלָם,
אֲשֶׁר קִדְּשָׁנוּ בְּמִצְוֹתָיו וְצִוָּנוּ עַל
נְטִילַת לוּלָב.

Praised are You, Adonai our God, Ruler of the world, who makes us holy with commandments and commands us to take the lulav.

2 When you shake the *lulav*, hold it in your right hand, with the *etrog* (stem, *pitam*, facing up) in your left hand. Bring them together and prepare to shake them three times in all directions.

3 Shake them in front of you, to the right, behind you, to the left, up, and down.

Shake That Lulav!

As we shake the *lulav* and *etrog* in all directions, we are reminded that God is all around us. Invent a brief dance or movement that expresses this idea. Incorporate the motions of shaking the *lulav* and the *etrog* into your movement in some way.

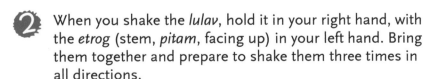 Draw three sketches of a stick figure doing the steps of your movement sequence below.

The S'chach: A Natural Covering

The sukkah's rooftop covering, called *s'chach*, is made out of materials that once grew in nature but are no longer attached to their life source (branches cannot be connected to trees, grasses cannot be connected to the ground, etc.). *S'chach* is often made of evergreen branches, cornstalks, or bamboo.

Imagine that you stepped into a sukkah with a roof of man-made materials. How might that feel different than one with a natural roof?

Do you think *s'chach* adds to the beauty of a sukkah? Why or why not?

Look at this sukkah created for Sukkah City, a design competition held in New York City in 2010. Through its use of simple materials, this sukkah's design emphasizes its impermanence. It is made of plywood, marsh grass, and twine.

Nature Walk

Take a nature walk and gather materials suitable for *s'chach* that you find along the way. As you walk, take time to notice the world around you. Listen to the wind, feel the ground beneath your feet, seek the beauty that can be found in the simplest of places. Bring a small bag, and use it to collect objects that you will use to create a piece of temporary art.

You might look for: Small twigs • Slightly larger branches that have already fallen off the tree • Leaves of different shapes, colors, and sizes • Bark that has already fallen off a tree • Grasses • Small stones/rocks • Flowers

Fractured Bubble by Henry Grosman and Babak Bryan, Sukkah City, 2010

Nature Art

Lay out the materials you have collected, and choose which ones you'd like to use to create your temporary artwork. Hold the materials in your hand. What do they feel like? What do they smell like? Find an outdoor space to work, and begin to arrange your objects. See if your objects suggest a natural design or shape that you can work from. Once you have created your work, take a photograph and leave your art behind. Wind, rain, animals, or other elements will slowly take your artwork apart.

Glue a photograph or draw a sketch of your nature art on the next page.

My Artist Statement

This piece is titled: _____

I felt _____ when I left my artwork behind

because: _____

This piece reminds me of Sukkot because _____

Peer Review

Ask a friend to respond to your artwork.

Name: _____

I noticed: _____

I appreciated: _____

I learned: _____

FINAL REFLECTION

Look back at the work you created in this chapter.

Which piece of art did you most connect with or enjoy?

What idea explored in this chapter resonated with you the most? Why?

How did the work you created lead you to think about Sukkot and the theme of protection?

Circle Dance by Tom Friedman, 2010

*"It is a Tree of Life to those that hold fast to it,
and all of its supporters are happy."*
—from the Eitz Chayim prayer

THE HOLIDAY of Simchat Torah immediately follows Sukkot. On Simchat Torah, we finish reading the Torah. Then, to demonstrate that our learning is ongoing, we immediately start the Torah cycle again by reading the very first chapter of the Torah. We celebrate with dancing, singing, and waving flags in the synagogue.

Gallery Tour

Tom Friedman (born in 1965) is an American artist. His sculptures are highly inventive and often use everyday materials, like Styrofoam, foil, paper, clay, wire, or plastic.

Look at this sculpture installation.

What do you notice about the placement of the people and their body positions? _____

_____

What do you think they are doing? _____

_____

What is one word or phrase you would use to describe this artwork? _____

_____

Have you ever seen people move like this? When or where?

_____

 Good to Know

The Torah is comprised of the Five Books of Moses. It takes one full year to cycle through reading the entire Torah, beginning and ending on the same day, Simchat Torah. Some congregations read one-third of each Torah portion at a time, so it takes them three years to complete reading the entire Torah.

 In the space below, draw as many circles as you can, along with other images that you associate with wholeness or completeness.

 Think About

A circle is closed, with no beginning and no end. It has no rough edges or sharp corners. For this reason, the circle is often used in art as a symbol of completeness. On Simchat Torah, our reading of the Torah is like a circle, with no beginning or end.

Dancing with the Torah

On Simchat Torah we carry the Torahs around the synagogue. Each circuit is called a *hakafah*. In between the *hakafot*, we dance joyfully around a Torah in the center of the circle. Though the artwork we just explored was not made to represent the way in which we celebrate on Simchat Torah, our dancing looks very similar to the circle of people shown in the sculpture.

In small groups, create your own *hakafah*. Hold each other's hands and make a circle. If you'd like, you can dance, too!

A Hidden Message

The Torah is filled with hidden meanings that we don't always see right away. For example, the last word of the Torah is *Yisrael* (Israel), and the last letter is *lamed*, ל. When we cycle back to the beginning of the Torah, the very first word we read in Genesis is *b'reishit* (in the beginning), and the very first letter is *bet*, ב.

When you combine the last letter and the first letter of the Torah, you get the word לֵב, *leiv*. *Leiv* means "heart."

What message is the Torah sending us when we end and then begin the Torah cycle with the word *leiv*?

How would you explain the connection between Torah and heart?

Write your thoughts here: _____

_____

We recite the following blessing when we are called to the Torah:

בָּרוּךְ אַתָּה, יְיָ אֱלֹהֵינוּ, מֶלֶךְ הָעוֹלָם,
אֲשֶׁר בָּחַר בָּנוּ מִכָּל הָעַמִּים
וְנָתַן לָנוּ אֶת תּוֹרָתוֹ.
בָּרוּךְ אַתָּה, יְיָ, נוֹתֵן הַתּוֹרָה.

Praised are You, Adonai, our God, Ruler of the world, for choosing us from all the nations and giving us God's Torah. Praised are You, Adonai, who gives us the Torah.

Think About

How can reading the Torah over and over again help us to make the lessons of the Torah a part of our lives?

On page 25, create a drawing that includes both a Torah and a heart, and shows something about the relationship you described. Use whatever materials you'd like.

A Tree of Life

The Torah is often called an *Eitz Chayim*, a "Tree of Life." At the conclusion of every Torah service, we recite this prayer:

It is a tree of life for those that hold fast to it, and all of its supporters are happy.
Its ways are ways of pleasantness, and all of its paths are peaceful.

Think About

How is the Torah like a tree? What makes up the trunk of the tree (the core of Torah)? What are the branches that extend to the sky? What are the roots?

Megillat Esther by Hirsch ben Leib Schlimowitz, 1879. This bear is filled in completely with the text of *Megillat Esther*.

VIDEO LINK: Creating a Micrography

About Art

Micrography is a folk-art technique in which an image is made entirely out of words. Sometimes the words create the outline of the image; sometimes they fill the center of the image and are written over and over.

Make your own micrography. First draw a large, simple outline of a tree in light pencil. Make sure there is a lot of empty space inside the tree for you to fill with words. You can use the words of the Eitz Chayim prayer, and then add your own words to fill in additional space. Consider changing your text colors to match elements of the picture. (If your words are in the trunk, use brown; in the leaves, use green). Use fine-tip markers or very sharp colored pencils for best results.

My Artist Statement

This piece is titled: _____

This piece is about: _____

I chose to use these words/quotes because: _____

Peer Review

Ask a friend to respond to your artwork.

Name: _____

I noticed: _____

I appreciated: _____

I learned: _____

FINAL REFLECTION

Look back at the work you created in this chapter.

Why do you think we reread the Torah every year?

Which ideas that you explored in this chapter were the most meaningful to you?

SHABBAT
Peaceful Rest

The Sleeping Gypsy by Henri Rousseau, 1897

"Shabbat has a flavor of paradise about it."
—Talmud *B'rachot*

SHABBAT is a twenty-five-hour period of time that we carve out of our hectic, daily lives and set aside as different from other days. It begins every Friday, just before sunset, and ends after sunset on Saturday evening. During Shabbat, we take a break from the everyday and refresh our spirits. At its best, Shabbat can be a day of prayer, rest, and relaxation, a chance to spend time with family and friends.

Gallery Tour

French artist **Henri Rousseau** (1844–1910) was a self-taught painter, who only began painting seriously in his early forties. This painting is one of his most famous, and employs a dreamlike style.

Observe this painting.

What do you imagine is happening? _____

_____

How do the colors suggest a tranquil feeling? _____

_____

What other elements in this painting make it look restful? _____

What surprises you or interests you about this painting? _____

Shabbat M'nuchah

Shabbat m'nuchah (rest) can mean a lot of different things, but at its most basic, it is about taking time away from the normal, everyday things you do and recharging. Like a minivacation, taking time for *Shabbat m'nuchah* each week can revitalize your spirits.

▶ VIDEO LINK: Zen Doodling

On page 31, draw a Zen doodle using a black or other dark marker. Draw lines across your page to create many small sections within it. Fill each small section with a different repeating pattern. Continue until your whole page is filled with different patterns.

Think About

On Shabbat, some people do not draw or color or do anything that is considered creating or destroying. Therefore, this activity is one that can be done in preparation for Shabbat or to help you think about relaxation in your own life. In what way can this activity relate to *Shabbat m'nuchah*? In what ways is this activity different from *Shabbat m'nuchah*?

About Art

The repetitive act of drawing simple shapes over and over again can foster calm, relaxing feelings.

A sample Zen doodle:
Miracles in the Desert
by Freddie Levin, 2016

Not sure what patterns to use to fill in your design? Here are some ideas.

Fill in each section with squiggles, waves, lines, or patterns.

Connect teardrops—upside down, then right-side up.

Outline shapes with a series of small circles.

Make simple shapes and repeat them.

Make patterns like these:

Draw three horizontal lines, then three vertical lines.

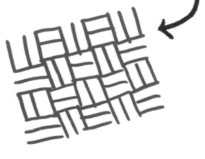

Make circles with two smaller circles inside. Connect them in rows.

Make a tic-tac-toe board, outline it, and fill in every other box.

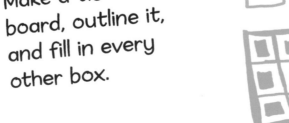

Make a box with a smaller box inside.

30

When you are done, trade books with a friend
and color in each other's Zen doodle.

A Day of Separation

What exactly does *kodesh,* or "holy," mean? It's a difficult idea. One definition of *holy* would be "separate." Keeping something separated from everything else is a way to express holiness. For example, we keep our holy objects separate from other objects: We keep our Torah in an Ark, we don't drink soda out of a Kiddush cup, and we don't use our challah covers as dishrags.

Shabbat is a holy day, so we separate it from other days by acting differently on Shabbat than we do at other times. We say prayers, eat special Shabbat foods, and rest. It's also a day we fill with rituals like lighting candles, making Kiddush, and eating challah. It's a separate, and holy, slice of time.

Kiddush cup from Jerusalem, 1908–29.

Below is a list of some holy objects and some ordinary objects. Next to each object, write the word *holy* or *not holy*. In the last column, explain your reasoning.

Object	Holy or Not Holy?	Why?
Kiddush cup		
Favorite baseball hat		
Jewish history book		
Torah scroll		
Challah		
Your baby brother or sister's favorite blankie		

What does holy mean to you? Write your own definition here: _____

About Art

Watercolor resist is a technique that uses watercolor paint along with another material, like wax or oil crayons, that doesn't mix with water and instead resists it. (Remember what happens when you try to mix oil and water? They separate.) For this technique, press firmly as you draw with crayons or oil pastels. Then, use watercolors, and paint right on top of your drawing. Wherever you have left a pastel mark, the paint will not stick, but will instead blend and flow around and behind the marks and into any open spaces on your page.

Planning your painting:

List three ritual objects that help you increase your own sense of Shabbat's holiness.

 _____

 _____

 _____

 VIDEO LINK: Painting with Watercolor Resist

Kiddush, which means holiness, is the blessing we recite over the wine or grape juice before a festive meal on Shabbat or other holy days.

בָּרוּךְ אַתָּה, יְיָ אֱלֹהֵינוּ, מֶלֶךְ הָעוֹלָם, בּוֹרֵא פְּרִי הַגָּפֶן.

Praised are You, Adonai our God, Ruler of the world, who creates the fruit of the vine.

Use oil pastels to create a drawing that depicts these three objects on pages 34 to 35. Think about where to place your objects—are they sitting on the ground? On a table? Are they floating in space?

Fill in some of the space with your drawings, but leave other space empty so that you can fill it with paint later. When you are done drawing, paint over and around your pastel lines with your watercolor paints. As you work, notice the way the oil pastels resist the watercolors. Just as oil pastels separate from watercolor, we use ritual objects to separate Shabbat from the rest of the week.

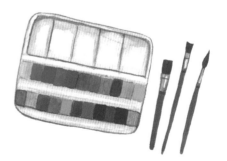

My Artist Statement

This piece is titled: _____

This piece is about: _____

I particularly liked using these images/elements: _____

_____

because: _____

Peer Review

Ask a friend to respond to your artwork.

Name: _____

I noticed: _____

I appreciated: _____

I learned: _____

Take a Technology Break!

Many of us rely heavily on technology and use it multiple times a day. Technology can be useful and fun, but it can also be draining. By separating ourselves from our devices for all or part of the twenty-five hours of Shabbat, we can give ourselves the opportunity to really experience the holiness of rest.

Create a Shabbat m'nuchah box.

Planning your project:
List at least three technology-free items that you can use to help you relax on Shabbat (pillows, books, etc.):

1 _____

2 _____

3 _____

Using self-hardening clay, create at least three clay models of objects that remind you of Shabbat or ways you want to relax during Shabbat. Once they are dry, paint the objects and your box with acrylic or tempera paint.

Think About

In what ways can displaying relaxing objects help you to enjoy Shabbat?

Create a rough sketch of each item in the space below:

 During the week, keep your items in your box. On Shabbat, take your items out and display them as reminders of how you might observe the day. You can also use the box to hold your phone, tablet, or other devices during your technology break.

Tape a photograph or make a drawing of your final items in the space below:

FINAL REFLECTION

Look back at the work you created in this chapter.

How do you feel about the idea that Shabbat can be a separate time for rest and relaxation?

How did the process of creating lead you to think differently about Shabbat?

Which ideas about Shabbat (holiness, separation, ritual, rest) did you find most meaningful? Why?

5 HANUKKAH
Light

ON HANUKKAH, we celebrate the victory of the Maccabees over the Syrian Greeks. Just as a small candle can illuminate the vast darkness, the small band of Maccabees was able to conquer the huge army of their oppressors. After their military victory, the Maccabees rededicated the Temple in Jerusalem and lit the Temple's oil menorah. Today, many families celebrate Hanukkah by lighting a *hanukkiyah*. We also eat foods made with oil, sing songs, and share gifts.

Gallery Tour

Yoram Raanan (born in 1953) is an Israeli artist. His paintings are a modern expression of Jewish ideas and often have a strong sense of light, color, and spirituality.

Look at this painting.

Choose a starting point and travel with your eye around the painting. What do you see? _____

_____

What colors does the artist use to create light? _____

_____

Spreading the Light by Yoram Raanan, 2017

38

How does the artist use brushstrokes and color to create the effect of glowing light? _____

_____

Light in the Darkness

On each night of Hanukkah we add another candle to our *hanukkiyah*, so that by the final night we have a full *hanukkiyah* glowing with light. Interestingly, there was a debate between two scholars in the Talmud, Hillel and Shammai. Shammai argued that we should start with eight lights on the first night, subtracting one each night, until on the last night, just one flame is lit. Hillel argued that we should start with one light, and add an additional flame each night, so that on the last night we have eight lights burning bright. We follow Hillel, always hoping to increase light to the world, not lessen it.

A copper *hanukkiyah* from Eastern Europe, eighteenth century

Good to Know

The word *hanukkah* means "dedication."

Think About

What do you think it means to add light to the world?

Blessings for lighting the *hanukkiyah*

בָּרוּךְ אַתָּה, יְיָ אֱלֹהֵינוּ, מֶלֶךְ הָעוֹלָם, אֲשֶׁר קִדְּשָׁנוּ בְּמִצְוֹתָיו וְצִוָּנוּ לְהַדְלִיק נֵר שֶׁל חֲנֻכָּה.

Praised are You, Adonai our God, Ruler of the world, who makes us holy with commandments and commands us to kindle the Hanukkah lights.

בָּרוּךְ אַתָּה, יְיָ אֱלֹהֵינוּ, מֶלֶךְ הָעוֹלָם, שֶׁעָשָׂה נִסִּים לַאֲבוֹתֵינוּ בַּיָּמִים הָהֵם בַּזְּמַן הַזֶּה.

Praised are You, Adonai our God, Ruler of the world, who made miracles for our ancestors in those days at this time.

(Shehecheyanu, the third blessing, is said on the first night of Hanukkah only.)

בָּרוּךְ אַתָּה, יְיָ אֱלֹהֵינוּ, מֶלֶךְ הָעוֹלָם, שֶׁהֶחֱיָנוּ, וְקִיְּמָנוּ, וְהִגִּיעָנוּ לַזְּמַן הַזֶּה.

Praised are You, Adonai our God, Ruler of the world, who has given us life, sustained us, and enabled us to reach this time.

Let the Light Shine Through

Working with a partner, make a top-ten list of songs that mention candles, light, shadows, or darkness.

1 _____

2 _____

3 _____

4 _____

5 _____

6 _____

7 _____

8 _____

9 _____

10 _____

About Art

Scratch art is created by layering bright or light colors underneath a layer of black or dark colors, then scratching the dark away to reveal the color beneath.

Think About

Why do you think light, or the absence of light, is something that inspires people to write songs?

▶ VIDEO LINK: Making Scratch Art

Comparing Cultures

In the Western Hemisphere, we celebrate Hanukkah in the winter months, when our world is at its darkest and coldest. At this time of year, the introduction of light is even more welcome and exciting.

Many other religions celebrate holidays at this time of year that use light symbolically. Can you name at least one other winter holiday in which light is central to the celebration?

Create a work of scratch art that shows how you can spread light or goodness in the world. Here's how: Using oil pastels or markers, fill in the box below. You can create a pattern or just fill in the space with sections of different colors. Then, using a black oil pastel (NOT a marker), cover the entire square with black. Finally, using a fine-point tool (toothpicks, or a plastic fork or knife), scratch your drawing into the black pastel. When you scratch out the black, the colors beneath should shine through.

Think About

What was your reaction to seeing the vibrant colors emerge from under the blackness?

The Story of Hanukkah

In the space below, you will find captions that retell the traditional story of the Maccabees. Add illustrations to each box about the story.

As you illustrate the story, think about the imagery and colors you use. The story starts out pretty dark but has a happy ending with lots of light. Can you illustrate your story in a way that has your panels go from dark to light?

 Good to Know

The Temple Menorah had seven branches. Our *hanukkiyot* have eight branches: one for each night of Hanukkah.

In the year 168 BCE, King Antiochus came to Jerusalem, stole from the Temple, and outlawed Judaism.

Mattathias cried out against the king,

Let everyone who is for God and Torah come with me!

Those that joined him were called the Maccabees.

The Maccabees were only a small group, while their enemy had a huge army!

When Mattathias perished in the fighting, his son Judah took over. The Maccabees fought bravely.

And they won!

The Maccabees cleaned up the Temple.

They ran to the Temple. When they entered, they were shocked by the destruction.

They named the new holiday "Hanukkah."

The Menorah stayed lit for eight whole days! The Maccabees decided to celebrate this miracle and their victory every year.

They could only find enough oil to last for one day but chose to light the Menorah anyway.

A Public Celebration

The rabbis of the Talmud tell us that we are supposed to light the Hanukkah candles in a public space, to share the light with the larger world. This reminds us that the Jewish religion was saved by the act of a small group of Jews standing up publicly for their beliefs.

At certain times in history it was dangerous to proclaim one's Judaism publicly, and displaying a *hanukkiyah* in one's window was unsafe. At those times, the rabbis decided that it was better to light the *hannukkiyah* inside or at the synagogue instead.

Gallery Tour

Louis Comfort Tiffany (1848–1933) is one of the most widely recognized American artists. He worked in a variety of media but was best known for his decorative glasswork, featured on stained glass windows and lamps.

Living Jewish Values

On Hanukkah, we fulfill the Jewish value of publicizing the miracle, *pirsumei nissa*, by making sure that our *hanukkiyah* can be seen by all by placing it in a doorway or window.

Stained glass window by Louis Comfort Tiffany, ca. 1880

About Art

Stained glass uses natural light for a beautiful effect. Because of the way light makes stained glass designs glow, stained glass is often used in religious settings, including synagogues and churches. Its glow is meant to symbolize goodness and holiness.

Think About

How do you feel about showing your Judaism in public today? For example, do you ever wear a Jewish star necklace or a T-shirt with Jewish slogans on it? Why or why not?

Make Your Own Window:

- Look at the window on page 44. Notice the thick lines separating each section of glass. These lines are typical of stained glass windows.

- Using the space on page 46, sketch out an image representing the light of Hanukkah. Use interesting lines to create different sections.

- With a black marker, trace your lines onto a transparency sheet.

- Use different colored permanent markers to fill in each of the sections.

- Once you have colored in all the sections, you can choose to use thick black puffy paint and retrace your black dividing lines. This will give your window a completed, three-dimensional look.

- Punch a hole at the top of your transparency sheet, and use a suction cup hook to attach your image to a window in your home or school.

- Take a photo of your artwork, and glue it in the space on page 47.

- Take pride in publicizing your artwork and your celebration of Hanukkah!

▶ VIDEO LINK: Making Your Own Window

FINAL REFLECTION

Look back at the work you created in this chapter.

Which piece of art did you most connect with or enjoy making?

In what ways did making the work push you to think more or differently about Hanukkah?

Which ideas about Hanukkah did you find most meaningful or relevant to you? Why?

My Artist Statement

This piece is titled: _____

This piece is about: _____

I particularly liked using these symbols: _____

because: _____

Peer Review

Ask a friend to respond to your artwork.

Name: _____

I noticed: _____

I appreciated: _____

I learned: _____

6 TU BISHEVAT
Nature

"Just as you found trees planted by others, you must plant for your children."
—*Midrash Tanchuma* on
Parashat K'doshim, chapter 8

ON TU BISHEVAT we celebrate trees and find meaning in nature. We plant trees and eat fruits and nuts that come from trees, particularly those commonly found in Israel. Some people observe Tu BiShevat with a seder meal in which they drink four cups of wine or grape juice symbolic of the four seasons, and eat different types of fruits, symbolic of different types of people. Many go on nature walks or plant seeds to get ready for spring.

Gallery Tour

This embroidered wall hanging was created in England in the seventeenth century. Although trees only grow one type of fruit, the artist of this piece chose to include many varieties.

Tree of Life (embroidered textile), seventeenth century

48

How many different living things do you notice in this work? Fill in the chart below (be as specific as possible), and compare your final list with your friends.

About Art

A listicle is a funny list that conveys an idea, like "top-ten reasons why . . ." or "the ten best things about . . ."

Animals I Notice	Plants I Notice	Other Things I Notice

In the space below create a listicle about trees. It could be the top-ten things you love about trees, your ten favorite uses for a tree, or the fifteen best reasons to celebrate trees today. See how ridiculous or funny you can make your list! Then, in groups of two or three, share your lists with your friends.

 Good to Know

The Torah teaches that for the first three years of a tree's life, you cannot eat any of the fruit that it produces. In ancient times, those who wanted to follow this law needed to know how old a tree was. Since it was impossible to track the actual birthday of every single tree, Tu BiShevat, a universal birthday for trees, was established. All trees were considered a year older on that day.

About Trees

Bal Tashchit: Avoiding Waste

Most of us, at some point or another, are wasteful. We don't always recycle, we buy more things than we need, and sometimes we let food go bad before we get a chance to eat it. Though this is certainly natural, it is helpful to think of the mitzvah of *bal tashchit*, "avoiding waste," as a guideline for taking care of natural resources.

Do you completely use every piece of paper before you discard it?

Do you repair your clothing and continue to wear it until it is too small?

Do you make sure to conserve food?

The mitzvah of *bal tashchit* comes from the Torah:

"When you make war against a city, and you have to lay siege to it for a long time to capture it, you must not destroy its [fruit] trees, wielding the ax against them. You may eat of them, but you may not cut them down."
—DEUTERONOMY 20:19

Based on this passage, the ancient rabbis taught that if we cannot cut down fruit trees in a time of war (when we might need them to make weapons), how much more so must we protect trees and the environment when we are not at war! The Talmud says, "Whoever breaks vessels, tears garments, destroys buildings, clogs wells, or does away with food in a destructive manner violates the idea of *bal tashchit*" (*KIDDUSHIN* 32A).

Tree of Life by Karla Gudeon

Think About

Is there such a thing as useful destruction?

50

In small groups, consider the following cases. Was the destruction in each case useful, or was it wasteful? Record your group's conclusions.

	Useful or Wasteful?
You strongly dislike the new shirt that you got as a gift. You put it away and store it in your attic.	
You have soccer cleats that are in decent shape but they no longer fit, so you put them in the recycling bin.	
You accidentally crack a dish, but you decide to use the pieces to make a mosaic.	
An abandoned building is knocked down in order to build a shelter for the homeless.	
A section of wetlands is drained in order to build a new mall.	

A Bal Tashchit Meditation

Find a comfortable spot, and close your eyes while thinking about the following:

Focus on a time when you were truly at home in nature. Imagine walking around, finding a comfortable place to sit. Where are you? What do you see? What does it smell like? How do you feel? Breathe in the fresh air. Breathe out the fresh air.

Now, think about a time when you felt that nature was being unnecessarily destroyed. Imagine walking around. Where are you? What do you see? What does it smell like? How do you feel?

Visualizing Bal Tashchit

In the space to the right, create a work of art that compares enjoying nature with destroying nature. Using web resources, old magazines or newspapers, or other materials, find images that represent both ideas, and use them to complete the page.

ENJOYING NATURE

Think About

Since Tu BiShevat is also about passing on ideas and resources to the next generation, consider ways you can share your ideas and creations with someone else.

 Using found and recyclable materials, create a piece of art that expresses your own thoughts on *bal tashchit*. Think about how you can use your materials and words to share your ideas about taking care of the environment and being responsible for the way we consume our resources. When complete, take a photo of your art, and paste it to the box on this page.

▶ VIDEO LINK:
Making Art from Found Objects

 **About Art**

Upcycling is a way of making art from found and recycled objects.

A Tu BiShevat Hike
Leave Nothing but Footprints, Take Nothing but Pictures

On Tu BiShevat, we focus on planting for the future. Take a nature hike with an eye toward appreciating the trees that were planted before you were born. Bring a camera on your hike, and take a variety of photographs. Remember, don't leave anything behind, and take only pictures!

A Tu BiShevat Journal Page

Print out one of the photos you took on your walk, and attach it in the middle of the next page. Notice that the page is divided into three sections. In the first section, write down as many words or phrases as you can think of related to your experiences on the hike. In the second section, doodle pictures that show how you can help protect our resources. Fill the third section with anything you choose: a poem about trees, more pictures, or a text from Jewish tradition about trees.

About Art

When taking photographs, choose interesting angles. Don't put your main image in the center of your frame; look at it from below, above, or around a corner. Try to make your photos look interesting by taking them from far away or very close up. Take one looking up from the ground or looking down at the smallest object on the ground. Use the camera to help you see things differently.

▶ VIDEO LINK: Making a Journal Page

In Glacier National Park
by Ansel Adams, 1942

55

Planting for the future

My Artist Statement

This piece is titled: _____

This piece is about: _____

I particularly liked using these images/words/elements:

_____

because: _____

Peer Review

Ask a friend to respond to your artwork:

Name: _____

I noticed: _____

I appreciated: _____

I learned: _____

FINAL REFLECTION

Look back at the work you created in this chapter.

How did encountering nature affect your views of Tu BiShevat?

In what ways can the Tu BiShevat holiday push us to think about our natural world?

What idea or theme explored in this chapter was most meaningful or relevant to you? Why?

⑦ PURIM
Speaking Up

Esther Denouncing Haman to King Ahasuerus by Ernest Normand, 1888

"Go, gather together all the Jews that are present in Shushan, and fast for me; neither eat nor drink for three days, night or day. I and my maidens will fast likewise; and so I will go to the king, even though it is against the law. And if I die, I die."

–Book of Esther, 4:16

PURIM celebrates the Jewish people being saved from Haman's deadly decree. On Purim, we share a meal with friends and family, exchange gifts of food, and read *Megillat Esther*, the story of Purim. Throughout the story, evil (Haman) and incompetence (King Ahasuerus) threaten to destroy the Jewish people. In contrast, we learn about Mordecai and Queen Esther, who were willing to stand up for what they believed in and are examples of bravery.

Gallery Tour

Ernest Normand (1857–1923) was a British painter who often painted historical scenes and portraits from Eastern and Middle Eastern cultures.

Look carefully at this painting.

Describe the scene shown in this painting. _____

_____

Who seems to have the most power? _____

_____

Who seems to have the least power? _____

Who is afraid?_____

_____

Who is courageous? _____

_____

What do you see that makes you think that? _____

_____

True courage is about doing what is right and having the strength of heart to get it done, even when you are afraid or unsure. Throughout the *Megillah*, we find examples of characters demonstrating moral courage—or doing the opposite. Each character's actions have significant consequences.

Living Jewish Values

The Jewish value of *ometz leiv* means "moral courage."

 VIDEO LINK: The Purim Story

Throughout the Purim story we find characters who are very ambitious and willing to go to extremes to get what they want. In some cases this is good; in other cases it is problematic. Think of how each of the following characters below did or did not demonstrate *ometz leiv* to get what they wanted. Give an example from the story to back up your answer.

Purim Character	Demonstrates Moral Courage?	Example from the Story to Back Up My Answer
Queen Vashti		
King Ahasuerus		
Mordecai		
Queen Esther		
Haman		

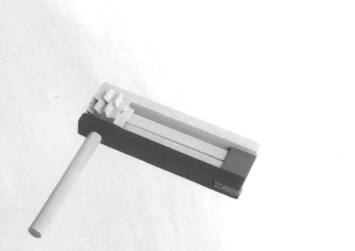

An Ometz Leiv Haiku

Choose one of the characters listed on page 59 and write a haiku poem describing how they did or did not demonstrate *ometz leiv*.

Here's a sample Haiku

Queen Esther's so cool
See how she turned the tables
And fought as a Jew

_____

_____

_____

About Art

A haiku is a traditional Japanese unrhymed poem consisting of three lines with seventeen syllables, written in a 5-7-5 syllable count.

Blotting Out Hate

During the traditional reading of *Megillat Esther*, we gather together to listen to the story. Since we are taught that Haman represents evil, every time the name Haman is read, we try to blot it out by making as much noise as we can: shaking noisemakers (*gragger*s), booing, stamping our feet—whatever we can think of!

On the next page is a triangle representing Haman's hat. Fill it in with as many injustices as you can think of. These can be things that bother you personally (bullying), or things that we encounter as a society (poverty, racism, etc.).

Once you have filled it with negative words, blot those words out with a dark marker. Scribble, make x marks, draw hard lines—just get rid of the words! (You can even use rubber stamps and an ink pad to stamp them out!)

Good to Know

On Purim, we eat *hamantashen*, cookies that are in the shape of triangles. They are meant to remind us of the triangular hat that Haman wore.

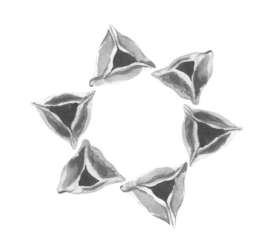

Think About

How does it feel to blot out all of those evil things? How is this similar to shaking a *gragger* during the *megillah* reading?

Rabbi Israel Salanter (1810–1883) once said, "When I was young, I wanted to change the world. I tried, but the world didn't change. So I decided to change my town, but my town didn't change. Then I resolved to change my family, but my family didn't change. Then I realized that I first had to change myself." When we think about blotting out the terrible problems we encounter in the world, it can feel overwhelming. Consider Rabbi Salanter's statement.

Why do you think it is so hard to change the world around us?

_____

What are some things you might be able to change in yourself that can help change the world? _____

_____

1 What is an issue that is important to you, that you would like to draw attention to?

2 Why did you choose this issue to focus on?

3 Draw a sketch that represents the issue.

4 Write a catchy slogan, rhyme, or saying that draws attention to your issue.

About Art

Artists throughout history have used the visual image as a tool to educate, to make people think, and to stand up for what they believe in. Resistance art is artwork that makes a statement and furthers conversation about an issue or problem.

A war protester holding a protest sign at a peace march in Washington, D.C.

The Gragger Project

Create a *gragger* that also is a piece of resistance art.

1 Take a cereal box that is completely empty and clean. Place a few handfuls of noisemaking materials, such as beans or coins, inside the box. Seal all the openings shut with duct tape. Cover the box with construction paper.

2 Plan your design around the issue you explored on page 63.

3 Using paint or markers, decorate your box with the slogan and images that represent the issue. They should describe the wrongs that you would like to blot out. Make sure you design all the sides of your box.

4 When it is complete, glue a photo or draw a picture of the front and back of your resistance *gragger* in the spaces to the right:

5 Bring your resistance *gragger* to synagogue on Purim.

▶ VIDEO LINK: Creating a Resistance Gragger

Front of my resistance *gragger*.

My Artist Statement

This piece is titled: _____

This piece is protesting: _____

I used these images/words/elements to depict the issue: _____

_____

because: _____

Peer Review

Ask a friend to respond to your artwork.

Name: _____

I noticed: _____

I appreciated: _____

I learned: _____

FINAL REFLECTION

Look back at the work you created in this chapter.

Which work of art or idea was the most meaningful or relevant to you?

In what way did the art you created in this chapter change your thinking about Purim or its themes?

How did the role of the *gragger* help you to think differently about ways you can affect the world?

Back of my resistance *gragger*.

8 PASSOVER
Freedom

"In every generation, each of us must think of ourselves as though we personally came out of Egypt"
—Passover Haggadah

THE FOCUS of our Passover celebration is the seder, at which we retell the story of the Exodus from Egypt and try to imagine that we were once slaves and were personally freed. We try to appreciate the freedom that we enjoy today, and have compassion for those who are not yet free and still suffering under oppression.

Gallery Tour

Moshe Castel (1909–1991) was an Israeli artist. His family was descended from Spanish Jews who immigrated to Palestine after the expulsion of the Jews from Spain in 1492. His murals currently hang in the Knesset (Israel's Parliament) and in Rockefeller Center in New York City.

Passover Carpet by Moshe Castel

Look at the work of art made from carpet

What part of the Passover story do you see in this work of art?

_____

_____

What part of the Passover celebration do you see in this work of art? _____

_____

_____

Take note of the Hebrew on each side of the artwork. On the bottom right it says *B'tzeit Yisrael* (when Israel left [the land of Egypt]), which refers to the Exodus. On the top left it says *Ha Lachma Anya* (this is the bread of affliction), the invitation at the beginning of the seder to "Let all who are hungry come and eat." What is the connection between the two panels? How does one side relate to the other?

How did the artist use color and line to connect the two different scenes into the same work of art?

_____

_____

Living Jewish Values

Over and over—thirty six times!— the Torah reminds us that we were once slaves in Egypt and therefore must have compassion for and take care of those less fortunate. The Torah is filled with lines like this: "You shall not wrong a stranger or oppress him; for you were strangers in the land of Egypt. You shall not mistreat any widow or orphan. If you harm them in any way—I will hear their cry as soon as they cry out to Me" (EXODUS 22:20-22).

Carving of bound slaves, Egypt

Historically, it was very difficult for widows, orphans, and strangers to support themselves, and so they relied on the generosity of others to make ends meet.

If we can use our history to inspire us to take care of those who are less fortunate than us, then we have understood the heart of what it means to be Jewish.

My Mitzrayim

The Hebrew word *Mitzrayim* means Egypt. However, *mitzrayim* can also be translated as "a narrow place." We escaped from Egypt; we escaped from a narrow space.

One way that people connect to the past is by relating the past to their own lives.

Using Moshe Castel's work as inspiration, create two works of art. In the narrow space on this page, depict a way in which you feel restricted. Then, in the wide space on page 69, depict a way in which you feel free. Look back at the way Moshe Castel used color to help differentiate the sections of his work. Do the same in your artwork, using one background color to represent restriction and another to represent freedom. Outline your images with marker and fill them in with crayons, oil pastels, or even paint.

My Artist Statement

These pieces are titled: _____

These pieces are about: _____

I particularly liked using these images/words/ elements: _____

_____

because: _____

Peer Review

Ask a friend to respond to your artwork.

Name: _____

I noticed: _____

I appreciated: _____

I learned: _____

It is not always easy to put ourselves in other people's shoes—even if they are our friends! It is that much more difficult to try to remember a story that happened thousands of years ago. Think of a time when you felt like a stranger—when you didn't know anybody—or a time when you did not feel welcome. Write about that time here. Then, trade books with a friend, and respond to their story while they respond to yours. (If you would prefer not to trade books, that's OK too.)

Why do you think the Torah wants us to remember the Exodus as if it happened to us?

Peer Response

Ask a friend to read your story.

(written by _____):

From reading this story, I learned: _____

_____

I feel _____ that my

friend had to go through _____

_____

If I had to go through that event, I would

have felt: _____

If I had to go through that experience I

might have done: _____

_____

I would like to tell my friend: _____

_____

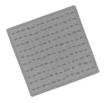

Empathy and the Passover Story

Try to imagine the emotions or sensations associated with the events of the Passover story. What were the people involved feeling as these events occurred?

Good to Know

Understanding someone else's emotions is called empathy.

Event	Emotions being felt
Moses's mother when she realizes she has to give up her baby	
Pharaoh's daughter when she finds baby Moses	
Moses when he realizes that he is an Israelite instead of an Egyptian	
Moses when he hears God speak to him from the burning bush	
Pharaoh when Moses demands that he let the Israelites go free	
An Egyptian sitting in pitch black after God unleashes the plague of darkness	
A slave child hearing that God is going to free him or her	
An Israelite walking across on dry land as the sea is split in two	
An Israelite dancing on the other side of the sea after escaping to freedom	

Empathy Squares: Abstract Art

Take a look at the two abstract pastel drawings below. Label them with an emotion or feeling, and explain your thinking. In each, line and color is used to depict a feeling. Are the lines dark and jagged? Are they smooth and rounded? Do they flow together or do they work against each other?

I think this drawing represents this emotion: _____

_____

I think this because: _____

I think this drawing represents this emotion: _____

_____

I think this because: _____

About Art

Instead of recognizable images, abstract art uses color, line, and shape to make a point.

Label each box on the next page with an emotion based on the Passover scenes on page 71. Then, using chalk or oil pastels, create an abstract image using color, line, and shape to represent that emotion.

My Artist Statement

This piece is titled: _____

The emotions I chose to depict are: _____

_____

I particularly liked using these images/words/elements: _____

_____

because: _____

Peer Review

Ask a friend to respond to your artwork.

Name: _____

I noticed: _____

I appreciated: _____

I learned: _____

FINAL REFLECTION

Look back at the work you created in this chapter.

Which projects or Passover themes were most interesting or relevant to you, and why?

Did any of the projects help you to empathize with the Israelites at the time of the Exodus? With people today?

"Remember . . . Do not forget!"
(Deuteronomy 25:17–19)

THE HOLOCAUST was a tragedy of epic proportions. On Yom Hashoah, we learn about the Holocaust and remember those who perished.

It can be uncomfortable to talk about the Holocaust, but art can help: Often works of art, such as the one featured here, are more capable of conveying difficult ideas than words alone.

Gallery Tour

Menashe Kadishman (1932–2015) was an Israeli sculptor and painter. His work often made use of steel cutouts.

This work is found in a hallway of the Jewish Museum Berlin. It is made up of more than ten thousand steel faces that completely cover the ground. Visitors must cross this hallway (and therefore MUST step on the faces) to get from one part of the museum to another. The steel faces make clanking noises as you step on them.

What emotions do you think the artist was trying to evoke in creating this piece? _____

Shalekhet (Fallen Leaves) by Menashe Kadishman, 1997–2001

How would you feel if you had to walk through this hallway?

_____

Would it have been as effective to create a wall hanging depicting the many faces instead of placing them on the floor? Why or why not? _____

_____

Being an Upstander

There are many stories from the Holocaust of people who did not stand by and allow their Jewish neighbors and friends to be taken away. These people, who some call "righteous gentiles," stood up and acted. Some of them opened their homes and businesses and hid Jewish people. Others took in Jewish children or worked to help Jews escape by providing them with documents or money.

Today we call brave people who come to the defense of others "upstanders." When bullies try to pull people down by making them feel unsafe or unwanted, upstanders stand up and make sure that those who need protection are not alone.

Think About

What lesson can we learn from the righteous gentiles who risked their lives to save Jewish people?

Upstanders Journal Page

In the boxes on the next page, create two stick-figure scenarios. In the first box, pick a setting (like the playground, a classroom, or the gym) and draw a stick-figure picture depicting "Life without Upstanders." (For example, your image could include bullies getting their way or kids getting hurt with nobody helping.) In the second box, draw a stick-figure picture called "Life with Upstanders." Draw the same image as the first box, but this time imagine what it would look like with one or more upstanders around to help.

In the space around the boxes, write a story about a time when you were an upstander, when you saw an upstander in action, or a time when you really needed an upstander. In your writing, include answers to the following questions: What happened? Who needed help? Who did the helping (if anyone)? How did you feel during the situation?

LIFE WITH UPSTANDERS

LIFE WITHOUT UPSTANDERS

My Artist Statement

This piece is titled: _____

This piece is about: _____

I can be an upstander by: _____

_____

Peer Review

Ask a friend to respond to your artwork.

Name: _____

I noticed: _____

I appreciated: _____

I learned: _____

Reclaiming the Jewish Star

During the Holocaust, Jews were singled out and marked as different from the rest of their countrymen. They were forced to wear a yellow star marked with the word *Jude* (Jew). This star was meant to humiliate Jews and ensure that they were easily recognized and identified.

Today, thankfully, the Jewish star is a symbol of pride, and many Jewish people choose to wear necklaces, T-shirts, or bracelets with Jewish stars to show their joy in their tradition.

For this project, create a Jewish star that reflects positivity and pride in Jewish life.

Cut out a Jewish star from cardboard and add your images to it. Each point should include an image that shows the positive associations you have with Jewish life. What do you like to do that is Jewish? What celebrations, ritual objects, events, or stories make you feel proud to be Jewish? Finally, use paint/puffy paint, gemstones, glitter, or any other materials you have to decorate your star.

When your star is dry, punch a hole in the top and hang it as a wall hanging.

Attach a picture of your Jewish star here:

FINAL REFLECTION

Look back at the work you created in this chapter.

Why do you think we choose to remember the Holocaust, such a tragic event in Jewish history?

In what ways can celebrating being Jewish today honor the memory of those who suffered or were killed in the Holocaust?

10 YOM HA'ATZMA'UT
Home

YOM HA'ATZMA'UT, Israel Independence Day, is a joyful holiday celebrating the creation of modern-day Israel. The reestablishment of a Jewish state in the ancient Jewish homeland is something that many have prayed and hoped for for thousands of years. Israel is a country that celebrates Jewish holidays, organizes itself around the Jewish calendar, and maintains Jewish culture and traditions. Any Jewish person is welcome to become a citizen of Israel.

In Israel on Yom Ha'atzma'ut there are many street festivals, concerts, picnics, cookouts, and parties throughout the country. At night, there are fireworks displays. In America, we celebrate Yom Ha'atzma'ut by marching in parades, eating Israeli food, and having parties in our homes, community centers, or synagogues.

Gallery Tour

Susan Gardner is an American artist living in Brooklyn, New York. She began creating this mosaic on the front of her home in 2001. It is made of shells, beads, buttons, broken dishes, tiles, mirrors, toy pieces, and more.

Mosaic House by Susan Gardner. Begun in 2001, still in process.

Look at this work.

What are some details you notice? _____

What three words would you use to describe this home? _____

78

The artist continues to add more detail to her piece—it is never complete. How does this affect how you view this work? _____

_____

Bless This Home
A Birkat Habayit Project

A *birkat habayit*, a "blessing for the home," describes the best things about home or the wishes one has for his or her home and the people in it.

Compare the work of art by Susan Gardner with the *birkat habayit* poem, below, by Julie Wohl. How are they similar? How are they different?

Create a *birkat habayit* that describes some of the things that you love about your own home. It could be the place where you spend time with family and friends, the place in which you are comfortable, or the place where you celebrate special occasions.

Kein Yehii Ratzon,
by Julie Wohl

Here is an example of a *birkat habayit*:

May this be a home filled
with laughter and love,
Health, joy, and contentment.
May all who enter know joy and all
who leave know satisfaction.
So may it be God's will.

The Hope for a Home

For many centuries, the Jewish people dreamed of the homeland described in the Torah and hoped for a place where all Jews would be safe and welcome. On May 14, 1948, when the nation of Israel was born, Jews the world over celebrated the realization of that dream.

The Jewish Homeland

Many Jews consider Israel to be their homeland, even if they do not live there. Some have family living there, and others feel connected to their ancestors who came from there. Some say that Israel is home because it is a country in which the people speak Hebrew. Others say that it is home because it is a country that uses the Torah as a guide for its ethical behaviors. Still others say they feel it is home because the landmarks they read about in the Torah are real places they can visit in Israel.

Like any home, our relationship with Israel can be complicated. It is a real place and, therefore, has many real problems. Arab Israelis don't always feel equal or welcomed, and Jewish citizens from different backgrounds often disagree with each other about what Israel should be like, how it should be governed, or even what land should be included within its borders. These disagreements can be very big, and people who live both inside and outside of Israel, and who care deeply about the country, often argue over what Israel means or over its government's actions. Nevertheless, on Yom Ha'atzma'ut we all celebrate together.

Comparing Cultures

In some ways, Yom Ha'atzma'ut is similar to the Fourth of July in America; in other ways it is very different. Fill in this Venn diagram, considering the similarities and differences between Yom Ha'atzma'ut and the Fourth of July. As you answer, think about how and where we celebrate, and the personal experiences of people who lived through independence.

80

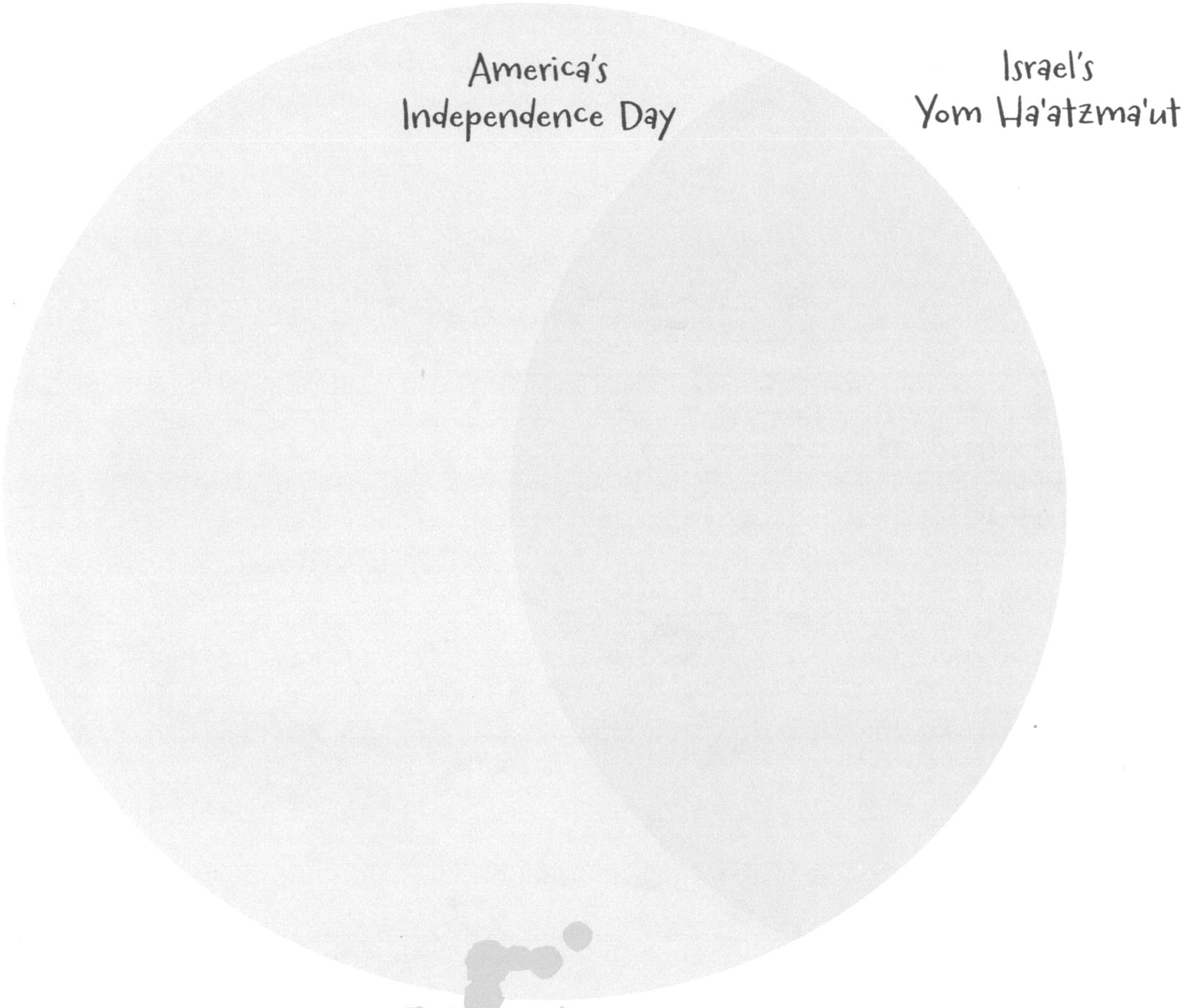

America's
Independence Day

Israel's
Yom Ha'atzma'ut

Symbolic by Design

The Israeli flag was designed by David Wolffsohn in 1897 as a symbol for the Zionist Congress. The Zionist Congress was a gathering of people from different countries, each dedicated to the goal of establishing a Jewish state. After much debate over what the flag should look like, Wolffsohn tells this story about how he came to his design idea:

> What flag would we hang in the Congress Hall? Then an idea struck me. We have a flag—and it is blue and white. The tallit (prayer shawl) with which we wrap ourselves when we pray: that is our symbol. Let us take this tallit from its bag and unroll it before the eyes of Israel and the eyes of all nations. So I ordered a blue and white flag with the Star of David painted upon it. That is how the national flag, which flew over Congress Hall, came into being.

Design an Israeli Flag Mosaic

On page 84, design a new version of the Israeli flag, and fill it in with small pieces of blue and white paper, so that it looks like a mosaic. Why a mosaic? Think about how Israel is a nation made up of people of many different religions, cultures, ideas, nationalities, even languages. Each person contributes to the whole; their diversity is the nation's strength. In a mosaic, as in any strong nation, the whole is greater than the sum of its parts.

To make your mosaic, use blue and white papers from a variety of sources (construction paper, scrapbook paper, tissue paper, online images, magazines, junk mail, calendars, old books, greeting cards). Cut them into small shapes and glue them down to create your new flag design. For design inspiration, consider using ideas or images related to the tallit, the Star of David, Israeli geography or landmarks, or Jewish ritual objects and symbols.

Twelve Tribes Mosaic, by Yael Portugheis, Jerusalem

About Art

A mosaic is made from a variety of small materials, often stone or glass, organized in such a way that when combined they create a larger work of art.

▶ VIDEO LINK: Making a Paper Mosaic Collage

My Artist Statement

This piece is titled: _____

This piece is about: _____

I particularly liked using these images/words/elements: _____

_____

because: _____

Peer Review

Ask a friend to respond to your artwork.

Name: _____

I noticed: _____

I appreciated: _____

I learned: _____

"Hatikvah": The Hope

The unofficial national anthem of Israel is "Hatikvah." The word *hatikvah* means "the hope." Read the words below and think about the idealistic hopes and ambitions that many people have for the modern state of Israel.

Gallery Tour

"Hatikvah" was originally a poem written by Naftali Herz Imber and first published in 1886. Imber was born in Galicia (now Ukraine) in 1856 and began writing poetry at age ten.

Hatikvah

As long as within our hearts
A Jewish spirit still yearns
As long as the eye looks eastward
toward Zion

Our hope is not yet lost
The hope of two thousand years
To be a free people in our land
The land of Zion and Jerusalem

Think About

How would you describe the hope referred to in the poem?

When you have to wait for a very long time before you get something, how does that affect how you feel when you finally get it?

In what way does it put a lot of pressure on the thing you want?

How do you think wishing for Israel for two thousand years has affected some people's feelings about it now that we finally have it?

▶ **VIDEO LINK: The Hope**
Listen to the music video of "Hatikvah" and write down your thoughts about Israel and hope.

The Real Israel: Embracing Imperfections

Now that Israel is no longer a dream and a hope but a real country with real people, it also has become a land with real disagreements and problems. Just like people in the United States have many disagreements about what the government's policies should be, this is also true of Israel. Some people want the country to be more religious, some less. Some people want the country to be more peaceful; others want it to stand up for itself and be stronger. These disagreements make it very clear to everyone that Israel is not a perfect place; but that imperfection does not mean we can't still have a strong connection to it.

A Japanese tea cup that was broken then repaired through the art form of Kintsugi.

About Art

The Japanese art form of Kintsugi, which means "golden repair," is the art of fixing broken pottery with a special lacquer dusted with powdered gold, silver, or platinum. Where some might throw away broken dishes or pottery, artists using Kintsugi use special glues to put the pieces back together. Because the glues are dusted with the gold, silver, or platinum, the places where the piece was broken are now the most beautiful parts of the work of art.

Think About

How might we look at Israel's imperfections in light of Kintsugi?

How might thinking about Kintsugi affect the way you view problems or disagreements in your own life?

In what ways can problems or imperfections (for example, people disagreeing with each other) be seen as positive rather than negative?

Making Art from Imperfection

Pass your art journal to a friend, and ask him or her to scribble on this page. When he or she is done, take your book back. Using markers or colored pencils, transform his or her scribbles into a beautiful piece of art. You can color in sections or add your own marks to make the scribbles into something else. Think about the lessons of Kintsugi: You can choose to see something as a "mess," or you can use the materials you have to fix it and make something beautiful, something that draws its strength from its messy parts.

FINAL REFLECTION

Look back at the work you created in this chapter.

How did thinking about the ideas of home affect your thinking about Israel?

What hopes do you have today for Israel?

11

SHAVUOT
Perspectives

*"One thing God has spoken;
two things have I heard."*
—Psalms 62:12

ON SHAVUOT, we celebrate the giving of the Torah to the Jewish people. This is no ordinary holiday, as the Torah is no ordinary gift! The Torah is the most significant foundational text of the Jewish people. Inside the Torah, we find our earliest history, our hopes and dreams as a people, and our basic values. The Torah connects us to our past and guides us on how to act as we move forward. It is the essential gift, and during Shavuot we make sure we show appreciation for that gift by using it the best way we know how: we study from it. We gather together in our community to learn— sometimes all night long.

Gallery Tour

Robert Delaunay (1885–1941) was a French artist who often used strong colors and geometric shapes. In this painting, he focused on how light streaming through stained-glass windows made the colors look as if they were constantly changing.

Simultaneous Windows on the City by Robert Delaunay, 1912

Think About

What is the best gift you ever received? Draw a picture of it in the box on the right.

How do we show appreciation for our gifts?

In what ways is the Torah like a gift?

If the Torah is a gift, what might we do to show our appreciation for it?

Look closely at this work.

Can you find areas in the painting in which the light shines in from different angles? _____

_____

If you did not know the title or background of this work, what might you think it was about? _____

_____

How does abstract art like this painting encourage different perspectives or ideas? _____

_____

 Good to Know

Some people study all night in what is called a *tikun leil Shavuot*. The act of studying Torah shows how much we appreciate the gift—we use it and we learn from it.

Living Jewish Values

It has been said that each verse of Torah can be interpreted in seventy different ways. This concept in Hebrew is called *shivim panim l'Torah:* The seventy faces—facets—of the Torah. In what ways does the concept of seventy faces compare to looking at abstract art?

Ripped-Paper Midrash
Make Your Midrash

Read the biblical story below. Then, make your own midrash, or interpretation of the story, using ripped paper:

And it came to pass on the third day, when it was morning, that there was thunder and lightning and a thick cloud upon the mount, and the voice of a horn exceedingly loud; and all the people in the camp trembled. And Moses brought forth the people out of the camp to meet God; and they stood at the foot of the mount.

Now Mount Sinai was altogether in smoke, because God had come down on it in fire; and the smoke rose up like the smoke of a furnace, and the whole mount quaked mightily.

And when the voice of the horn grew louder and louder, Moses spoke, and God answered him.

And the Lord came down upon Mount Sinai, to the top of the mount; and the Lord called Moses to the top of the mount; and Moses went up.—EXODUS 19:16–20

First, carefully analyze the text. Underline all of the dramatic images and effects that you would like to include in your artwork. Circle anything that you find perplexing.

Then, using only ripped construction paper and glue, depict your interpretation of the text in the space on page 92. Keep the following things in mind as you create:

What were the people feeling as they experienced the giving of the Torah? _____

_____

How big was the mountain compared to the people? _____

_____

Where was the smoke, fire, etc., in relation to the mountain and in relation to the people? _____

_____

How close do you think the people were to the mountain?

_____

Will you try to depict one person's experience or the experience of the whole group? Did everyone experience the same thing at this key moment, or did they each have different perspectives? _____

_____

About Art

A midrash is a story or insight that helps explain a challenging text in the Torah. Rabbi Jo Milgrom invented the technique of using torn paper to create a midrash, called a "ripped-paper midrash." When creating a ripped-paper midrash, the artist chooses, on purpose, to be spontaneous and imperfect. There is no precision: no cutting, measuring, or drawing. Instead, the artist is entirely focused on the meaning of his or her work.

▶ VIDEO LINK: Making Midrash

Think About

Compare your own work with the work of a friend. In what ways are they similar? In what ways are they different? How does this relate to the idea that there are countless ways to interpret Torah?

What lessons can we learn from the idea that there are seventy different ways to interpret each verse of Torah?

How might you apply those lessons to your own life?

FINAL REFLECTION

Look back at the work you created in this chapter.

Which ideas or artwork were most meaningful or relevant to you?

What new ideas about Shavuot did you learn from your friends?

My Artist Statement

The Torah describes the moment God gave the Ten Commandments this way: _____

I imagine that it looked like: _____

I imagine that it sounded like: _____

I imagine that the people felt: _____

Peer Review

Ask a friend to respond to your artwork.

Name: _____

I noticed: _____

I appreciated: _____

I learned: _____

12 PUTTING IT ALL TOGETHER

MAZEL TOV! You made it through the whole book, thinking, reflecting, designing, and creating all the way! Before you complete your journey, take a moment to look back at the portfolio of work you have created throughout this book. Review it, chapter by chapter, piece by piece, and think about what you've done. Do you want to add anything? Take anything away? Would you do anything differently if you were making the work now?

Take notes in the chart below and reflect. Be proud of what you have created!

Holiday	What Do You Notice about Your Work?	What Ideas Are Most Meaningful to You?	What Did You Most Enjoy?
Rosh Hashanah/Yom Kippur			
Sukkot			
Simchat Torah			
Shabbat			

Holiday	What Do You Notice about Your Work?	What Ideas Are Most Meaningful to You?	What Did You Most Enjoy?
Hanukkah			
Tu BiShevat			
Purim			
Passover			
Yom Hashoah			
Yom Ha'atzma'ut			
Shavuot			

Pass this journal to two friends. Ask them to make comments or observations about your work, and include them here.

Name: _____

I noticed: _____

I particularly liked: _____

I'm wondering: _____

Name: _____

I noticed: _____

I particularly liked: _____

I'm wondering: _____

Making Your Final Mark

As you completed these projects, you experimented with a variety of art forms and delved deeply into the meaning of the Jewish holidays. Using materials of your choice, create a collage or painting that shows what you think and feel about the Jewish holidays. You can use both images and words, and you can combine other media (newspapers, tissue paper, paint, pastels, markers, etc.) to create something unique.

My Artist Statement

The title of this piece is: _____

_____

It represents: _____

_____

Date of book completion: _____

Final thoughts: _____

_____

Printed in the USA
CPSIA information can be obtained
at www.ICGtesting.com
JSHW041352240823
47143JS00001B/1